CW00864389

Animals with Bite

Jaguar

by Julie Murray

Dash!
LEVELED READERS
An Imprint of Abdo Zoom • abdobooks.com

1

Dash!
LEVELED READERS

1

Level 1 – Beginning
Short and simple sentences with familiar words or patterns for children who are beginning to understand how letters and sounds go together.

Level 2 – Emerging
Longer words and sentences with more complex language patterns for readers who are practicing common words and letter sounds.

Level 3 – Transitional
More developed language and vocabulary for readers who are becoming more independent.

THIS BOOK CONTAINS RECYCLED MATERIALS

abdobooks.com

Published by Abdo Zoom, a division of ABDO, PO Box 398166, Minneapolis, Minnesota 55439.
Copyright © 2021 by Abdo Consulting Group, Inc. International copyrights reserved in all countries.
No part of this book may be reproduced in any form without written permission from the publisher.
Dash!™ is a trademark and logo of Abdo Zoom.

Printed in the United States of America, North Mankato, Minnesota.
102020
012021

Photo Credits: Alamy, iStock, Minden Pictures, Shutterstock
Production Contributors: Kenny Abdo, Jennie Forsberg, Grace Hansen, John Hansen
Design Contributors: Dorothy Toth, Neil Klinepier

Library of Congress Control Number: 2020910913

Publisher's Cataloging in Publication Data

Names: Murray, Julie, author.
Title: Jaguar / by Julie Murray.
Description: Minneapolis, Minnesota : Abdo Zoom, 2021 | Series: Animals with bite | Includes online resources and index.
Identifiers: ISBN 9781098223007 (lib. bdg.) | ISBN 9781098223700 (ebook) | ISBN 9781098224059 (Read-to-Me ebook)
Subjects: LCSH: Jaguar--Juvenile literature. | Big cats--Juvenile literature. | Cats--Behavior--Juvenile literature. | Bites and stings--Juvenile literature. | Predatory animals--Juvenile literature.
Classification: DDC 591.53--dc23

Table of Contents

Jaguar

Jaguars live in Central and South America. They can also be found in Mexico.

They live in mountains, forests, and deserts. They are often near water.

Jaguars are big cats. They can grow up to six feet (1.8 m) long. Their tails can be two feet (0.6 m) long!

Jaguars have strong legs. They are good jumpers and climbers.

Jaguars have tan coats with dark spots. The spots are called **rosettes**.

A jaguar's coat is good **camouflage** in the trees.

14

Jaguars are **ambush** hunters. They lie and wait quietly. Then they pounce on their **prey**.

They hunt deer, pigs, and birds.
They also eat fish and **reptiles**.

Jaguars have strong jaws.
Their bites are powerful!

More Facts

- Jaguars are good swimmers!

- There are around 15,000 jaguars living in the wild today.

- Jaguars are the biggest wild cats in the Americas.

Glossary

ambush – a surprise attack from a hidden place.

camouflage – a defense used by some animals to disguise their appearance, usually to blend in with their surroundings.

prey – an animal that is hunted by another animal.

reptile – a cold-blooded animal with a skeleton inside its body and dry scales or hard plates on its skin. Most reptiles lay eggs.

rosette – a marking with black spots encircling a center spot.

Index

Online Resources

Booklinks
NONFICTION NETWORK
FREE! ONLINE NONFICTION RESOURCES

To learn more about jaguars, please visit **abdobooklinks.com** or scan this QR code. These links are routinely monitored and updated to provide the most current information available.